I Like Sal

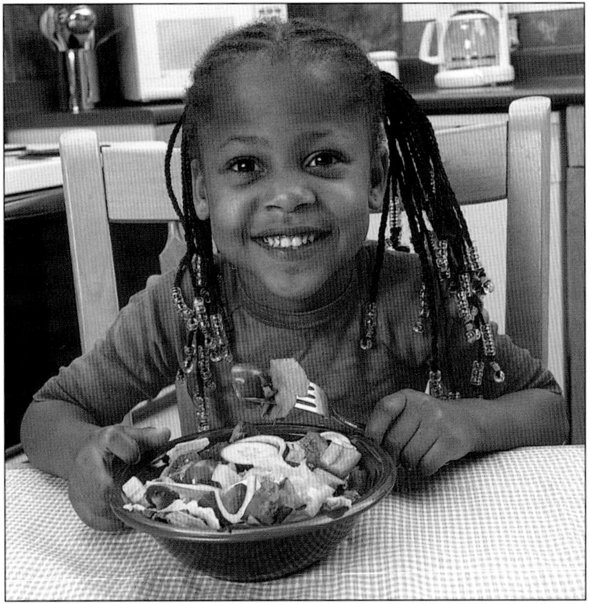

Christine Finochio • Jennette MacKenzie

I like lettuce.

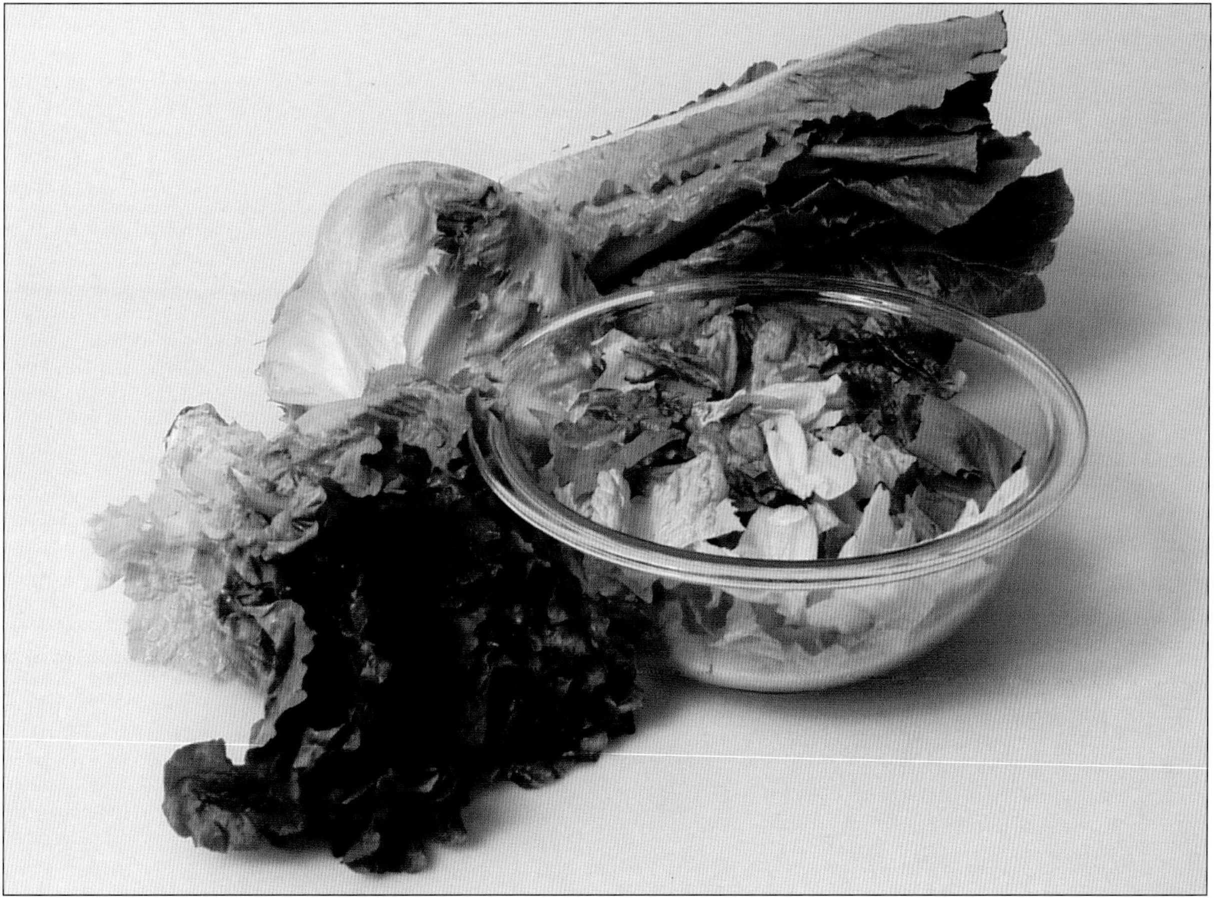

I like carrots.

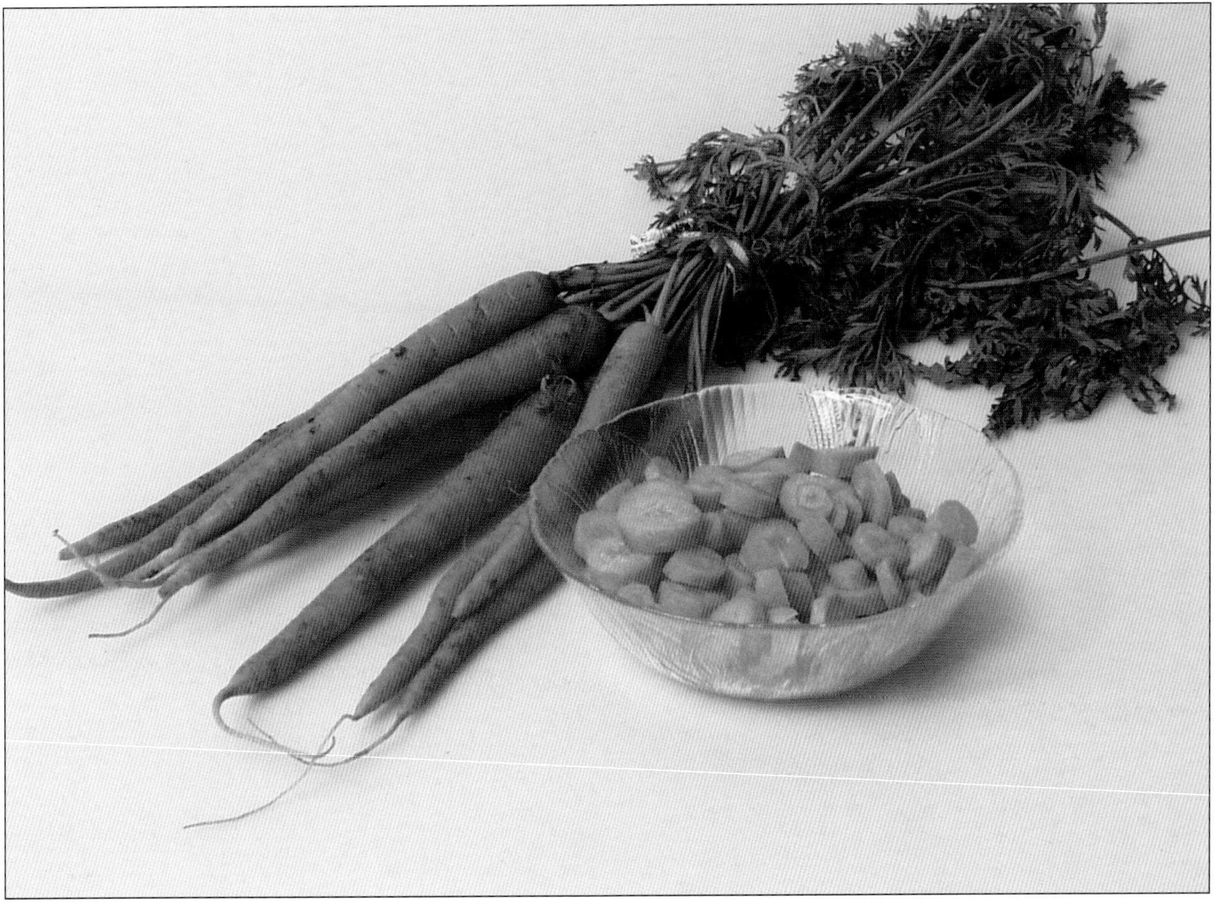

I like peppers.

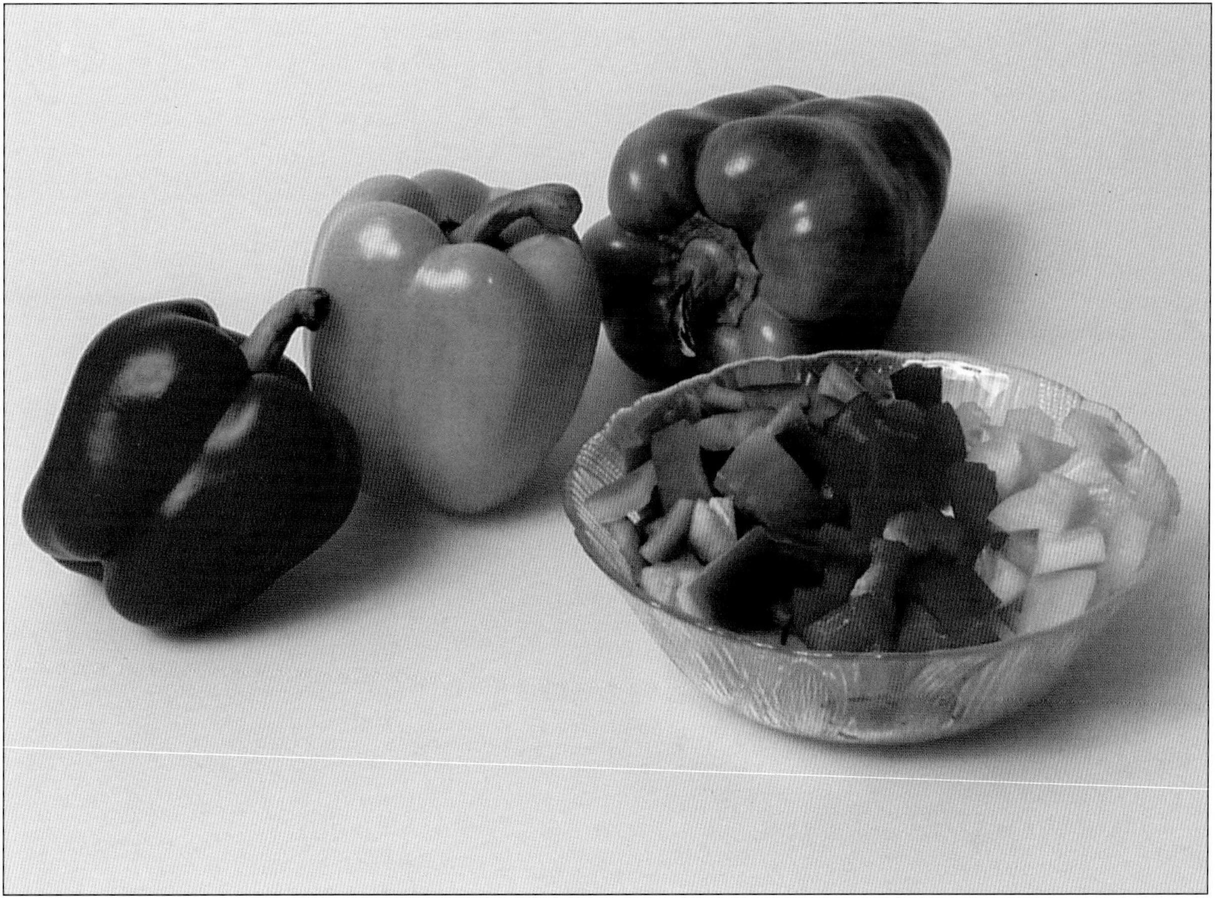

I like celery.

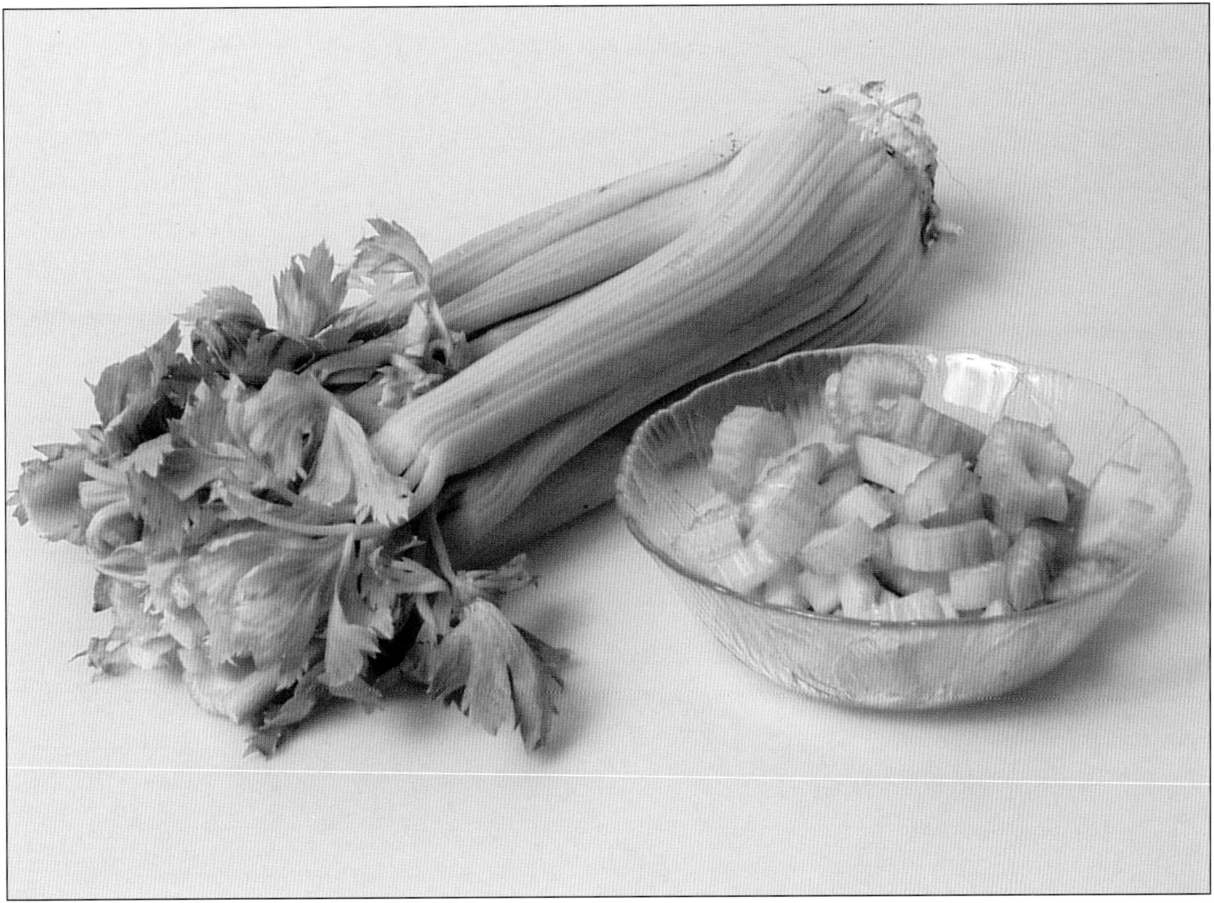

I like onions.

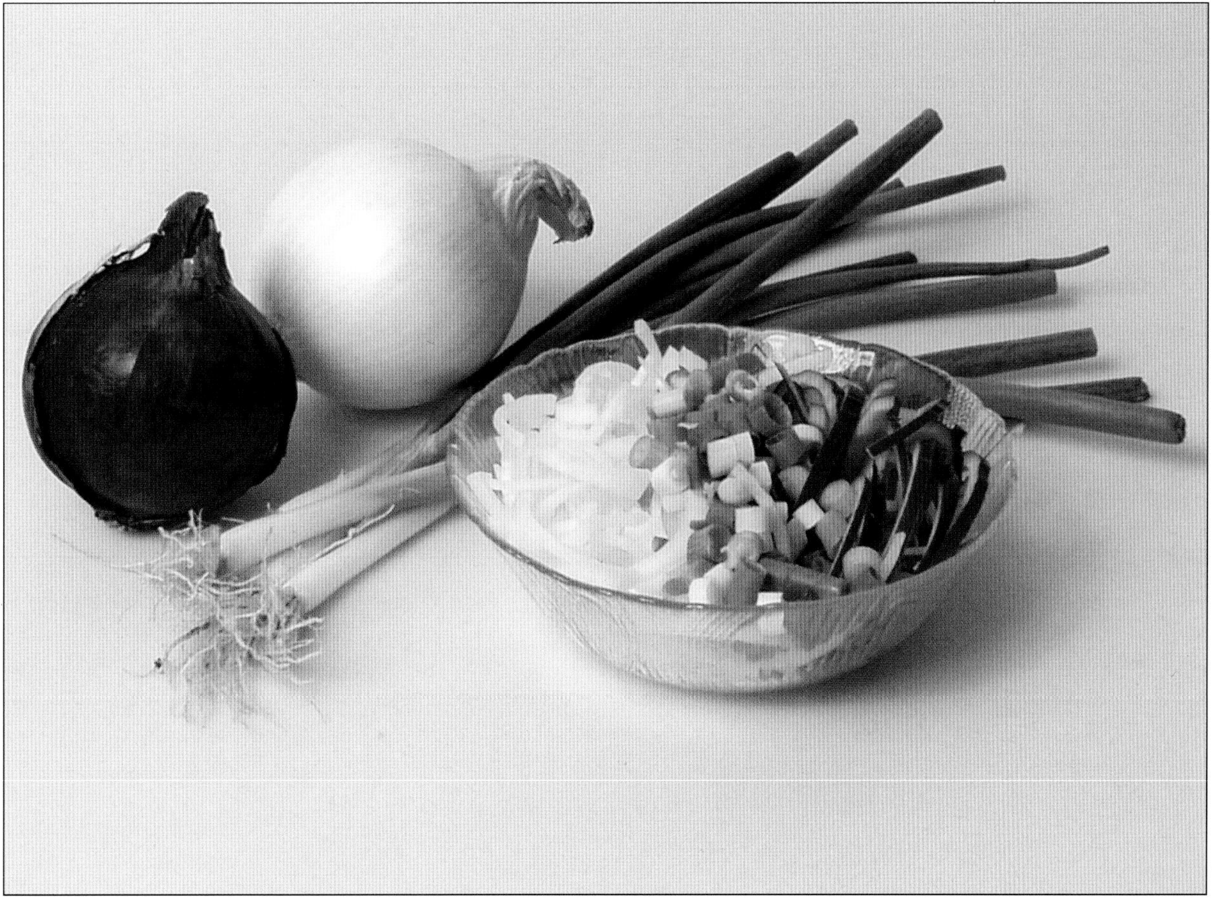

I like tomatoes.

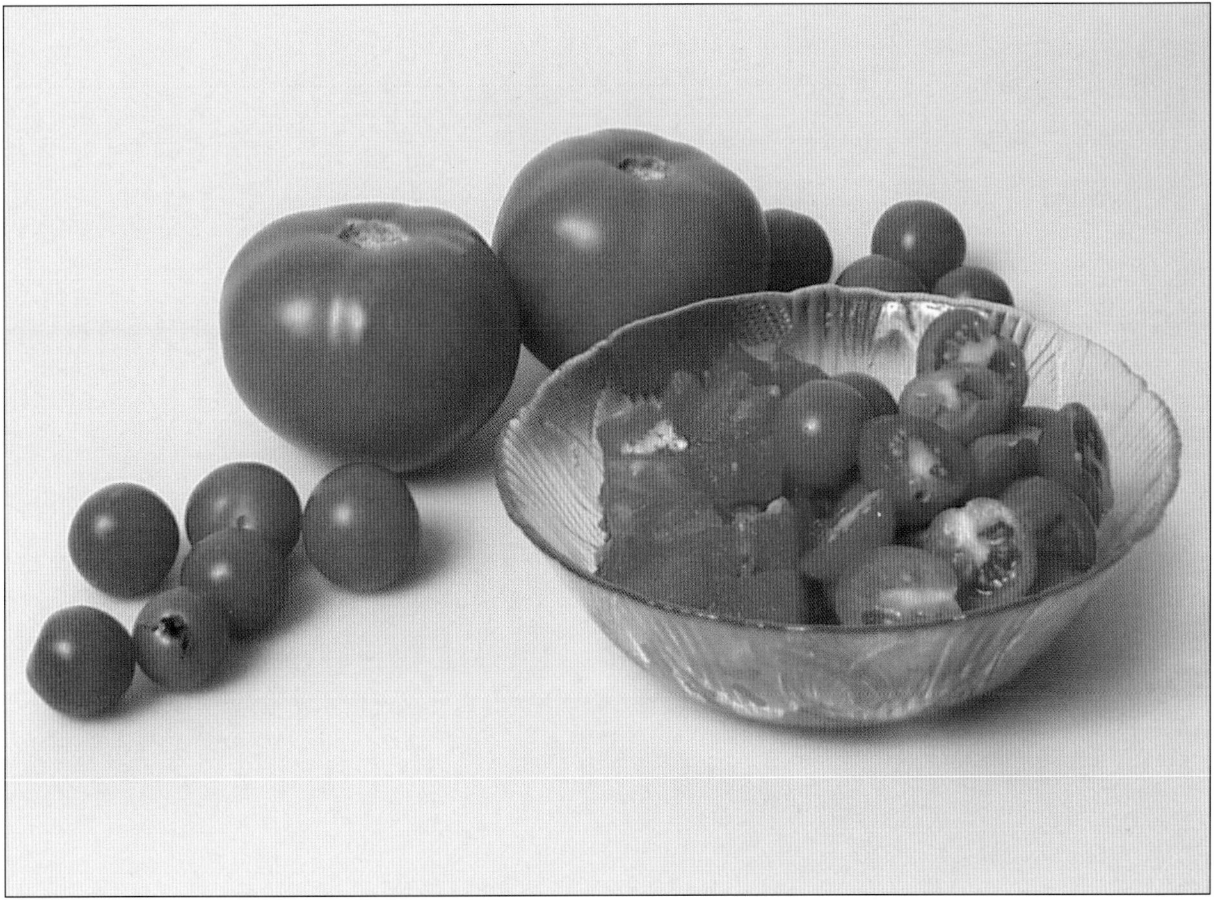

I like cucumbers.

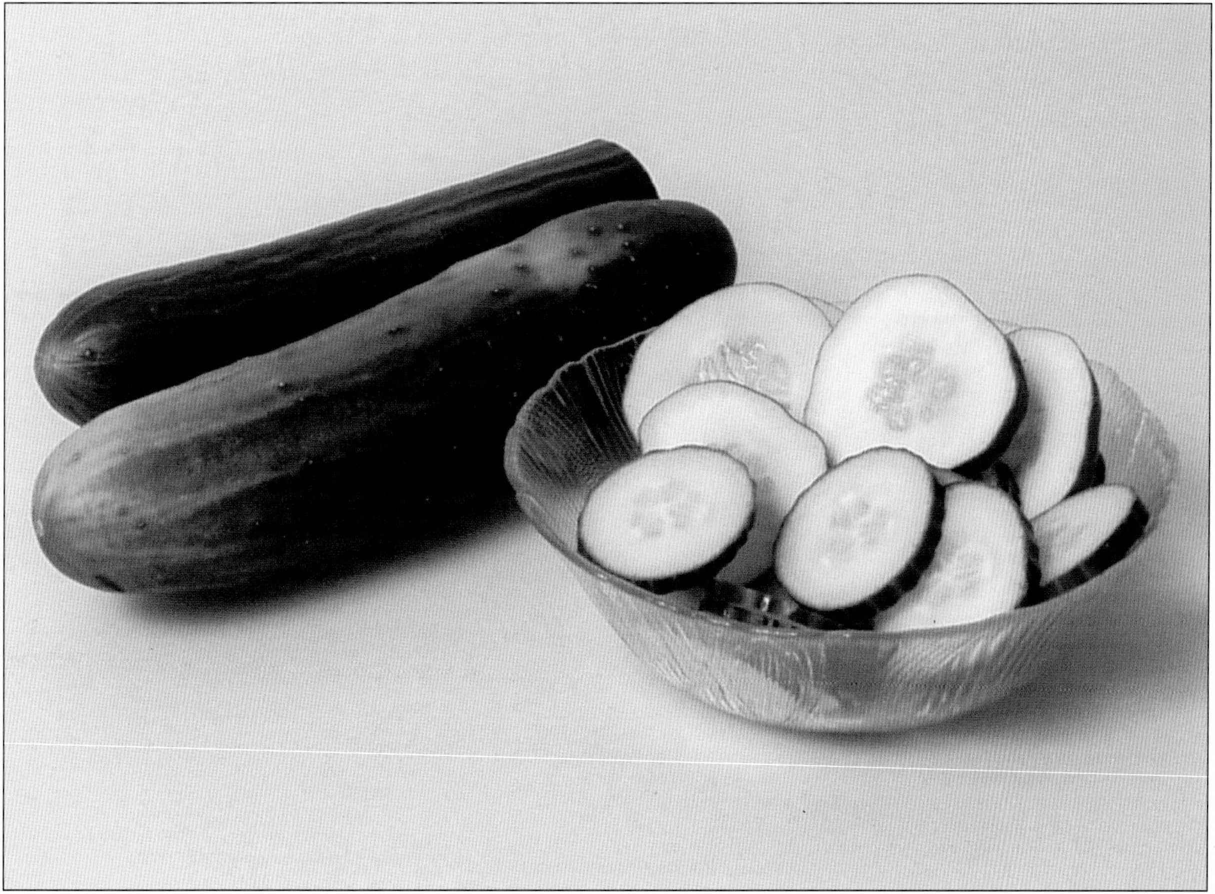

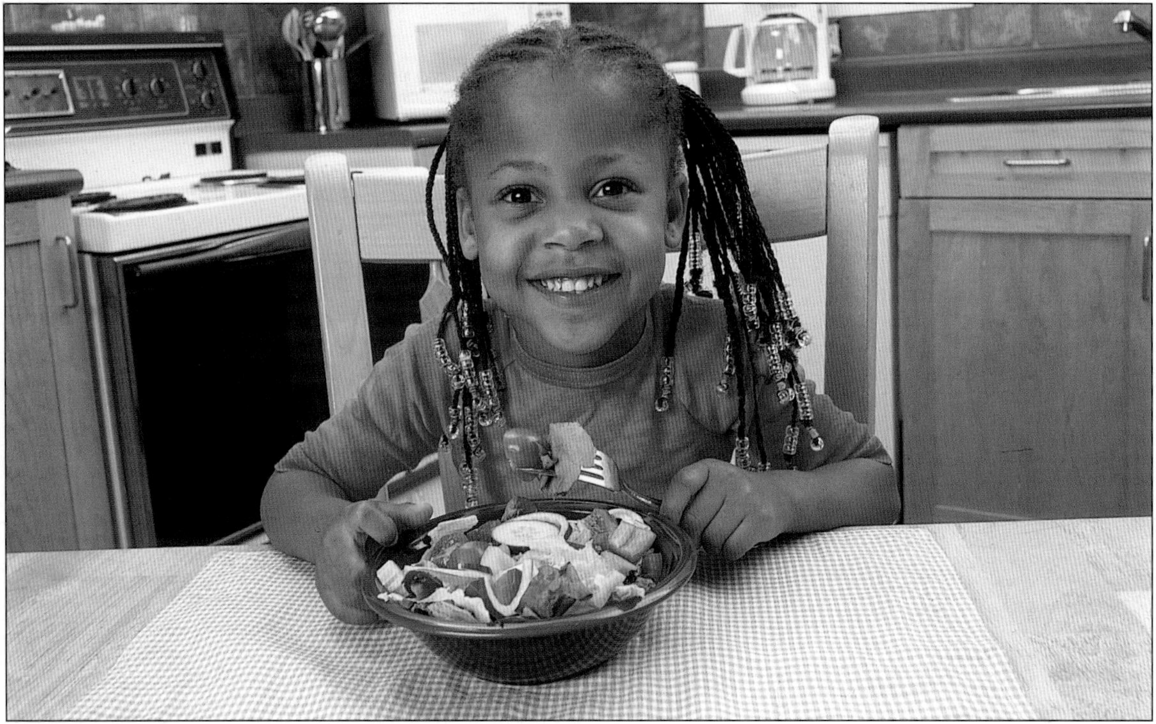

I like salad.